Standardizing Standard Operating Procedures

Standardizing Standard Operating Procedures

HOW TO WRITE THEM AND COMMUNICATE THEM, SO PEOPLE WILL FOLLOW THEM

Jerry Isenhour

© 2017 Jerry Isenhour
All rights reserved.

ISBN-13: 9781548579104
ISBN-10: 1548579106
Library of Congress Control Number: 2017910773
CreateSpace Independent Publishing Platform
North Charleston, South Carolina

Recommendations from some of the companies who have followed Jerry's systematized processes for composing SOPs & SOGs.

Outstanding job of creating "Everything you always wanted to know about SOPs but were afraid to ask" This is the quintessential guide to understanding how to write great SOPs and why they are key to eliminating chaos in your business. The title could have been "SOPs For Dummies"! Mastering SOPs and understanding your numbers are probably two of the most important things a business owner should focus on to insure success.

Chuck Roydhouse / The Roydhouse Effect

With this valuable little manual, Jerry takes what seems like an overwhelming task and makes it achievable. He explains why the small business owner needs SOP's and SOG's and then gives a step by step guide to developing, writing and implementing them. I've been overwhelmed by the process in the past, but now I'm excited. Thank you, Jerry!

Rudi & Georgette Oosting / Oosting Custom Masonry

I found this book to be very well written and easy to read. Good information for instituting procedures for your company, whether it is an established company or just starting out. Jerry has done a wonderful job in explaining the **"hows and whys"** of the importance of generating and implementing thorough operating procedures and guidelines.

Mark & Julie Dent / Chesapeake Chimney & Co.

One of the most impactful things we have done to build our marketing company into a 7-figure business is to get SOP's done at every level of our business. That would have never happened if we had not known Jerry Isenhour. It was Jerry who convinced us, after many months that this was a necessary step in the growth of our business and we will be forever grateful.

Carter Harkins & Taylor Hill / Spark Marketer

Whether you are just starting in business or looking for ways to streamline your processes, this is the book for you. Jerry clearly and concisely lays out step by step instructions for creating, utilizing, updating, and enforcing SOP's for every facet of your business. If you find writing SOP's to be daunting or just are not sure where to start, Jerry will guide you in his book. My company has been calling upon Jerry for many years to ensure our business is running at peak performance.

Jeremy & Brandi Biswell / Flues Brothers

One of the biggest frustrations of growing a business is the need to rely on employees to do what they are supposed to. Without established SOPs in place, the only result will be complete chaos and an owner shackled to every aspect to the business. By putting systems in place, the business owner can pass the many burdens of the business off to an employee; by properly training them, giving them a written formula for success, and a way to hold them accountable for what they are expected to do in every aspect of their job.

Jerry has developed a great approach for business owners to create systems, put them in writing, and creating a systematic machine. This is a process that is difficult to start, but once you get doing this on a continuous basis, it really becomes a new way to conduct business. I've used this simple system and it has given me so much more freedom from my business to grow it, and just step away with the assurance that my staff will do the right thing without me being there. Simply put; if you apply the simple principles laid out in this book, and continue to do it, your business will be much more manageable, enjoyable, and far less stressful. These are the reasons we started a business, right.

Steve Sobszak / Total Chimney Care & The Cozy Flame

As the owner of a franchise operation I was provided an entire operations manual with my franchise purchase. However, from consulting with Jerry I have been able to refine these into a systemized set of guidelines that fit my specific market and my specific business. Jerry's systems pay off for me in the leadership skills of myself and my team, along with being a key ingredient in building our company culture which helps us fulfill our company mission to my customers and community. After review of this book his concepts and principals are on track and on target, follow these guidelines and you can build your own systematized business. Thanks Jerry for your guidance and counsel.

Craig Williams / ServPro of West Mecklenburg

Contents

	Foreword · xiii
Chapter 1	What are Standard Operating Systems (Sops) and Standard Operating Guidelines (Sogs)? · · · · · · · · · · · · · · · · · 1
Chapter 2	How do I Get Started with the Sop Process? · 3
Chapter 3	Ok, I Have My List: Identifying Priority is Next · 8
Chapter 4	Ok, I Have My Prioritized List: What Now? · 11
Chapter 5	What do I Put into the Draft? · · · · · · · · 17

Chapter 6	Management Review of the Sop ······ 19
Chapter 7	Submit the Document for Editing ····· 21
Chapter 8	Test the Sop ······················ 23
Chapter 9	Submit the Sop to Your Team Members···················· 25
Chapter 10	Implementation of the Sop··········· 28
Chapter 11	Distribution of the Sop ·············· 30
Chapter 12	Inspect for What You Expect·········· 32
Chapter 13	What do I do When a Mistake Happens?························ 34
Chapter 14	How do I Apply Disciplinary Action Using the Sop? ·············· 37
Chapter 15	Ongoing Review and Suggested Modifications by Your Team Members···················· 39
Chapter 16	Annual Management Review·········· 41
Chapter 17	Summaries of the Sops ·············· 43

Chapter 18 Security of the Sop · · · · · · · · · · · · · · · · 44

Summary and Conclusions · · · · · · · · · · 45

About the Author · · · · · · · · · · · · · · · · · 47

Foreword

Standard operating procedures (SOPs) and standard operating guidelines (SOGs) are such important parts of the operating system for any company. However, at the same time, it is one of the hardest tasks the manager will ever undertake. The idea—which is used by the US military and successful businesses such as McDonald's and is a part of many franchise concepts—is a simple one. It is the process by which successful businesses mold their operations. It is the heart of any franchise. Why? Because a franchise promises you a proven business model, a business plan, and the systems by which to operate it daily. This desire for a turnkey business start up with a business plan is probably the main attraction for potential business owners to attend franchise fairs and to buy existing businesses: the ability to buy a business concept that has the systems the systems for operation and success spelled out.

This book contains guidelines for use by managers and management teams, including the *whys* and the *hows* of writing SOPs and SOGs for any business model. I compiled this process after years of writing these for my own companies, writing templates for others to work from and providing SOPs to company management for start-ups for existing businesses, and for those who are planning to exit their business and need the SOPs as an added value in the sale process. I have also provided numerous seminars on the subject showing the concept and the process. This book is a compilation of those methods. Without a system of SOPs and SOGs, the value of a business is difficult to determine, which means that the company does not show its real potential value for a prospective buyer if a sale of the business is considered, the systems will be a part of the sale value of the business.

A leading aspect of the SOP/SOG process—and the difficulty—involves the method of getting your team members "bought into" both the preparation of the SOPs as well as acceptance and compliance after the SOPs have been implemented. As you read this guide, you will find that I advise involving the staff in the drafting, editing, and approval process. An essential part of making this process successful is for all members of the team to be working together to accomplish the goal.

The SOP guidelines are created to facilitate the entire way you do business. They make things smoother and more effortless and help prevent mistakes. Because SOPs simplify and formalize every task, they also create the advantage that no process in your company rests solely in the hands of a single member of your team. The lack of SOPs creates a condition that if key people leave, their knowledge and expertise does not disappear with them.

STANDARDIZING STANDARD OPERATING

Without such systems, the business may inevitably by crippled by having an operational reliance on the expertise of a handful of people who are the only ones who know the "secret sauce" of the business model. Having SOPs and SOGs in place means you don't have to worry that the loss of key people could cripple your operation.

Systems should be composed with the result in mind; as you assemble the systems, they must be built for the goal size of the company, not just for the size of the company you operate today. By assembling the systems, you have created the formula to scale and replicate the business. Lastly, if the company were to be sold at a future time, your "secret sauce" (your processes) could well be the added value that would make your business much more desirable in the sale process, creating a quicker sale and a higher return for you. It could even be the deciding factor that the buyer decides that the business you are selling is one that will bring them the return they seek in buying the business.

Here is an explanation of why leadership, culture, and systems are three of the most important elements to business success:

Leadership: This is always the number one ingredient, no matter the company size, from one to one hundred to one thousand team members. No matter what the company size is, leadership is required. You may ask, "But if I have no team, why are leadership skills so essential?" The answer is simple: it takes leadership to lead customers. Your leadership skills will spill over to everyone you meet, including your potential customers. Also, leaders are commonly sought out by the people we want to do business with. It takes true leadership skills to accomplish this, and the same goes for your team. It takes a true leader to lead people; leaders easily lead followers, but leaders also must learn to lead leaders, a more difficult task. So, determine that leadership is a skill you will learn, nurture, and grow into. It will make a dramatic change in the outcome of everything you do.

Culture: Culture is the way we work and the way we present ourselves, our company, our products, and our services to others. Every team's goal should be to create a culture of excellence. When this kind of culture is evident, your customers will feel it, and success becomes an integral part of the entire business endeavor.

Systems: Systems provide the ties that bind it all together. Systems are the road map; they are the GPS by which we operate. There are certainly many skills that must be involved, but without a well-devised and meticulously structured system, we have chaos and the kind of operation that results in waste, creates inferior products and services, and has no way of tracking progress. Nor does it provide us the measurement tools required for a successful outcome each business day.

Before you delve into the subject understand that businesses commonly consist of processes that determine how the business operates, how a product is produced, how services are sold and how the product is delivered to the customer. This is also referred to as commerce, where the company produces or supplies a product (material or service) that is purchased by the customer and the customer, in turn, pays the supplying company for the products and services received.

STANDARDIZING STANDARD OPERATING

Often, the method or production will vary and will come from individuals who conceive their process to deliver the product. This was discovered by Henry Ford as he entered the automobile industry and began to produce automobiles for sale to the public. To produce the product properly, true to the design, where the result was the same each time, Mr. Ford developed the modern assembly line. This assembly line is an example of the wisdom of systems. The assembly line was how the automobile was first efficiently produced and how it came to change the lives of people all over the world, putting these methods to work can and will deliver to you a better product, produced in less time, with less waste of material and labor, and can deliver a product to your customer in a way that is to the plan and providing you with the highest return.

Lastly, understand that SOPs and SOGs are not job descriptions, they are not position agreements, rather the SOP / SOG is a task directive, it involves a single task, and in this we provide the guidelines by which the task is to be completed, and if the process is followed the result is the product/service is delivered on time, at highest quality, without waste and provides the customer satisfaction required for long term success and growth of the business.

CHAPTER 1

WHAT ARE STANDARD OPERATING SYSTEMS (SOPS) AND STANDARD OPERATING GUIDELINES (SOGS)?

Let's start by establishing what **SOP**s and **SOG**s, most importantly why do you need both?

It's quite simple:

The SOP is a step-by-step guideline how the task or job is to be done.

The SOG, on the other hand, is the explanation of why the job is to be done the specified way.

It is my opinion that the **SOP** and the **SOG** should be combined in the same document that we refer to for simplicity as the **SOP**. Both the **how** and the **why** are needed for a successful system to evolve. By having them in one combined document for each task, we have accomplished the important steps of both describing the task and detailing the reasons for it.

Without a thorough understanding of the reasoning for the **SOP**, the reader may fail to understand why this

SOP is needed and important. In simple terms, the **SOG** is the why, and the **SOP** is the how!

The ability to lead people in the 21st century as the generations change has now become a critical part of the leadership process, the culture process, and the systems processes. Not only must we provide a thorough understanding of the how of every task, today's world now requires that we provide the whys of each process. Why we do this the way specified as described, and includes the anticipated results if the process is not properly followed. Only by the proper explanation of the why with the importance of the process can one hope to construct the best system of processes to govern the systems of the business regarding all aspects. Quite simply, the generation of today, and into the future must now understand why.

As you read further, the abbreviation **SOP** will be used to encompass both the how of the **SOP** and the why of the **SOG**.

CHAPTER 2
How do I Get Started with the Sop Process?

Start with a list of every task to be done within the business. (+) Dept. No task is too small, nor is it unimportant. Each task is a part of the overall team effort of producing the best product or service that you can, and each part plays a role in this process. This list of tasks will grow as you go through the process; you will discover and uncover additional processes that require detailing in the SOP. Now, before going further, think about how many times in a week, a year, or maybe throughout your career you have been asked to answer the same question over and over and over. *[Question for group]*

Sit down at your keyboard, or at a writing table with a pen or pencil, and begin the process of recording your thoughts on a SOP. In doing this, you are moving that process from your mind to paper. Through this process, you'll be able to provide the details for any task you can think of—and that detail is what moves all tasks from a vague idea to a specifically designed, detailed and orchestrated procedure. ==Every needed process of the business should be adequately described with a SOP.==

By doing this, you are making a map of what is inside your head. The mapping of our thought process is often referred to as just that: mind mapping. Mind mapping is used in many universities and business think tanks to formulate complicated programs from the initial idea and turn it into a product. It's the process used to get the ideas to move from thought to actual design and then to testing and production. Mind mapping is like an outline but much more imaginative and detailed.

You can also use a whiteboard or flip charts, which may better enable you to review what you think once you have placed it on the paper or board. This formulation process may go on for a period; it could well be a list that is added to often. What you are doing is embarking on a long-term project in a way that can be later recalled, added to, amended, and whatever else is needed to make the result perfect.

==You might find it helpful to create categories within the company for this process.==

You can break the company into as many general categories as you wish. What you are writing is a worksheet for the SOP process. The map you are creating is intended to guide you on this journey into a steadier, clearer, and better flow for the work you do every day in your business life. This deep-thought stage is a time for free-flowing ideas.

Whatever method you use to record your mind map, you will have your beginning structure, an outline or use of mind mapping of your thoughts. It will give you the comprehensive road map to your final goal: a listing of how to perform the tasks required to make each day of your business life as productive and error-free as possible. Just imagine how much lower your stress level will be as you complete this process and it moves to implementation.

The road map will remain a part of growing your SOPs. Think of this as your operational listing for your business operations. It is the origin, but as we move forward, these beginning steps will later produce more evolved outcomes. Often people will take a digital photo of the thought processes to have available on a smartphone or tablet for recall when they think of an addition.

I highly suggest that the best way to build this project is to designate a wall where you can have the entire project laid out in front of you. This will be an ongoing project. Being able to view your thoughts in this manner will enable you to put together a comprehensive plan to move forward to the next steps. Having your map laid out and in view will help you to stay on track and keep your notes in a visible place. This is an important project, and it deserves the space to do it properly.

As discussed a wall with a large white board or a wall where the maps you are constructing can be displayed and seen is an excellent place to do your mapping of the project. Some also find the use of a flip chart is helpful in noting the various tasks and the needed contents of an SOP. Enabling you to survey the total plan will be both a tremendous time saver and will function to keep things on track and moving on schedule for your completion date.

Set goals for yourself and your team for the SOP production, instead of simply having a goal of producing SOPs, rather set up a weekly or monthly goal of how many you will complete in that time frame. Setting goals for this project, like any lofty goal, must be written and reviewed often to ensure you are on track. And along with this develop a system of measurement of your progress to ensure you are on target with the project to meet your goal completion date.

For this project to succeed goals are a requirement, but I caution you, many set the long-term goal, if SOPs are the goal, then they set a goal of building a library of task oriented SOPs, but often it does not happen. The reason? They set a single long-term goal, however for the process to work it requires a series of short term goals, as such I suggest you set your sights as follows. How many can you produce in a week? Or you may set a monthly goal.

As you begin the process, a beginning point will be explained as listing the needed SOPs for your business. Once that is done you may find you have 50, and perhaps you have 100, perhaps you have more. Once this is done many will find it to be a number that may appear to be incapable of producing. But if you found yourself with a long-term goal of producing 100 SOPs, it may simply make you think; I cannot do this. But can you do two a week? If so you will accomplish your goal in one year. If you did for a week, you could accomplish this in 6 months. If you wrote six a week, you could accomplish the task in approximately four months.

You should also plan to schedule your time for the process if you simply do these when the mood strikes, you will find that it quite simply will never get done. Remember the time spent on this task now will reward you with more time to strategize how to move the business forward in the future and not spinning your wheels over and over with the same issues, problems and frustrations day after day. Think of the SOPs as a time saving and money-making tool when completed.

CHAPTER 3

OK, I HAVE MY LIST: IDENTIFYING PRIORITY IS NEXT

The next step is the prioritization of the task list. I suggest you file the tasks into the categories listed below. It is also good if you start to color code the listings. The four categories you will divide into are:

Critical: The tasks included in this category are essential for the business to operate. In other words, you must have these, and you must follow them. All SOPs are important, but the ones in this category are the most critical to your business.

Very Important: These are items that, while very important, are not critical to the company opening each work day. However, even though these are not critical in that short-term time frame, they are required for the long-term success of the business.

Important: A task rated in this category will be one that is important, but not of paramount importance for business success daily. Nevertheless, do not let this stop you from writing these down. Remember all the little details of the business that you must explain every

STANDARDIZING STANDARD OPERATING

day; just think how much time you would save if these were written down where your team could refer to them instead of simply asking you. You can devote that time saved to begin devoting time to working on the business and enjoying the great things you want to do personally. Without documenting these details with the how you do it alga with why you are doing it, you are dooming yourself to a life of repeating them over and over.

Not Important: Just like in the "not as important" category, you will find there are minor tasks that must be addressed. We have prioritized these in a way to help you accomplish the creation of a total operating system for your business model.

As was discussed at the beginning of the chapter, color coding will make this a much easier process. The use of color will utilize both sides of your brain, which is a way of making sure you are providing a complete picture. The construction of your SOP program requires the complete functioning of both sides of your brain to thoroughly and completely accomplish this very detailed task.

The process for color coding is as follows:

Select a color for each of the four categories of priority. For example:

RED **Critical:** Is red a good color? When you list priority items, they could be in red, or any color that would identify these as critical to you.

~~red~~ **Very Important:** What color will key you to this, at a glance this color will automatically denote it as a Very Important item, not critical, but very important to success.

Orange

[handwritten: Yellow] **Important:** Select another color for these; any color will work, but it needs to be a color that at a glance says that it is an important factor.

[handwritten: Green] **Not Important:** Select the fourth color, any color will work if it can be noted as different from the previous three.

Once these categories are color coded, a quick glance at this chart will provide you with a visual image of the program in a way that more directly involves your mind. The color is a significant way to illustrate and divide the sections into manageable formats.

Now you may ask, how do I divide these? That is a decision only you and your team can decide, but prioritization of the tasks is highly important for you to obtain your objective.

CHAPTER 4

OK, I HAVE MY PRIORITIZED LIST: WHAT NOW?

Now it is time to gain assistance from other team members. You may have other capable people on your team you can enlist for the initial draft of the SOPs. If you are an existing business with team members, some of them may be better at certain tasks than you are. If you are in the building stage of the business, this may be a task you will have to handle alone. But if you do have a team, involve them; this is the start of the buy-in process, and by involving them it becomes something they will believe in, buy into and work with you to assure compliance. When there is a team, system building should be a team project, never a one-person project.

Whether you are a start-up or a small company, the importance of this task is high. If the business is to grow, the systems you are detailing in the SOPs will be the foundation of your business operations. You are also laying the framework for the culture of excellence that will be instilled as a part of the growth of the business model as it reaches your goal destination.

However, before you do that, let me offer some advice on getting everyone completely on board.

It is essential that management understands that for this process to work, the employees must buy into it. Otherwise, the SOPs you are writing will never become part of the daily operational protocol in your business. They will disappear like fog on a sunny day, and your team will revert to doing things the old way—their way— just because it's familiar.

Achieving this buy-in involves more than just including your team in the process of writing and reviewing each new SOP. That is just a mechanical process, like any other purely mechanical part of the job, and it does not necessarily lead to buy-in. Just because employees do something, it doesn't mean their hearts and minds are fully engaged, nor do they exhibit concern about the quality of the outcome. We all know this. That's one of the main reasons that when we hire new employees, the mating of our company core values to those of the people we hire is always a primary concern. We are, after all, trying to create a cohesive, committed team. We want a team of leaders, not followers. We want a team of people who give every task their full attention toward a common outcome. We want a team for whom this work is a profession, not just a job.

What buy-in means is that your team not only "gets" the whole idea, but they are also enthusiastic about the implications for them and the business once the system

Think of our Why

STANDARDIZING STANDARD OPERATING

is in place. This enthusiasm is not something they do just because you asked them to. It's not just another task to accomplish so they can move on. For this kind of buy-in—the kind that excites them and generates enthusiasm rather than just compliance—they'll need to be inspired. And the only one who can make that happen for them is the leader, and that is likely you!

To do that, we suggest having a company meeting where you explain the whole idea behind creating SOPs: to make sure that all tasks are performed in the same way no matter who is involved in the process. You should explain the reasoning behind the system development: it reduces the risk of mistakes, and it makes new personnel training easier for both the person doing the training and for the new hire. SOPs simplify communication because they remove confusion and eliminate the need to seek out management for clarity.

[margin note: Pre kickoff]

By having SOPs for every task, we eliminate wasted time and effort. The money saved in this process, which is often considerable, goes directly to our bottom line and is available for other uses more valuable to the business and everyone involved.

But, most importantly, having SOPs in place will make everyone's job easier because there will now be a comprehensive written and standardized method for every task required. This makes the team members more self-sufficient because no employee ever needs to check with management about how or why to do a task. Those questions have been addressed in the SOP if we have taken the steps of properly detailing. And because the team will

[margin note: Additionally, standardization!]

create, review, and approve these SOPs together, it virtually eliminates the chance that the SOPs will be unclear, unnecessary, or incorrect.

What you are building into this is a system of empowerment, where the team members are provided the guidance of how to make decisions, instead of delaying resolutions when issues arise. When a customer has a question, they want an answer, not a messenger that has to find someone else to take ownership of the problem. Companies that empower their teams to make decisions are those that are at the top of their field regarding customer service and other customer driven requirements.

In other words, SOPs are not just considered everyone's responsibility; they are also a win for everyone on the team if all team members buy into the process.

Once an SOP has been created and approved, it must be implemented and put into practice. That means it will become more than just a document. It will now be the officially approved method for doing any task relevant to the business, which means it will be how each task is completed, no matter who is doing it.

Proper implementation is a vastly important element of the process. It means that everyone not only is on board with the change but is committed to making it the standard practice. This is something we do as a team. This is how we make the business stronger, more successful, more productive, and more rewarding in every way. This is not something to be taken lightly.

Once the trial period of implementation is over, and everyone's input has been gathered and considered, whatever remaining issues there might have been with the SOP will have been entirely resolved. At that point, we will consider everyone fully committed to using the new procedure.

If this is not happening, then as the leader you must uncover the opposition and alleviate it. It will become an issue at a later point. An uncommitted team member can wreak havoc on the process with the team at a later point, most especially with new hires.

You should be following up to make sure that everyone is performing the task exactly the way it has been defined in the SOP. You must regularly follow up on your current procedures, inspecting for what you expect, to make sure all are doing the job properly and making the customer happy. If in the process of following up, we discover that an approved SOP is not being followed, unless there are significant extenuating circumstances, it will be considered cause for being noted in the employee's file as a violation, and disciplinary action. Obviously, that, or any other violation of company protocol, would be a serious event that could lead to dismissal if it were to be repeated. Failure to inspect for compliance should be viewed as a leadership failure, not a team failure: after all the leader let it happen, and it was on his watch!

If this SOP is describing a new task for your current company or if your company is a start-up, you may need to seek the advice of others regarding the details of the steps that will be involved. If you're taking that first step into self-employment, you may not yet realize all the tasks that will require documentation. If you're involved in a start-up business that you research the entire topic of business success. A common failure of many who enter the world of entrepreneurship is that they want to command the technical aspects of the product or service but overlook the infrastructure of the business. Often this turns out to be a fatal flaw that could lead to the failure of the business. To avoid this, you'll want to look at the mechanics of all sections of the business model.

When you attempt to enlist the aid of others on your team, some may feel unqualified due to their limited writing expertise or ability to transcribe this into a written draft. Assure them that they are not creating the final product; rather, you are seeking fundamental input on how to do the job properly. Assure them that this input from them is invaluable to the project's success. Many times, an expert in the process cannot write the details, as he or she fails to understand what a person who is inexperienced in the task does not know. It is common, that when a technical expert writes an initial draft, for it to require editing to be a successful document that a person inexperienced in the task can understand. The failure of many SOPs: they are written in such a way that a person inexperienced in the task cannot perform it based on the information contained in the SOP.

Remember, this is only the first draft of the SOP. There are other steps involved.

The bottom line is that you need to assemble an initial draft of the task. Often starting simply as an outline of the task and only later evolve into a more polished product as you move forward in the project.

CHAPTER 5

WHAT DO I PUT INTO THE DRAFT?

The draft must contain both the *hows* (how the task is done) and the *whys* (the reasons why we do it) and the importance of the task to our overall business success. Remember, it is a combination of both the SOG and the SOP. The reader of the SOP must be made to understand that, no matter how menial a task seems, it is an essential part of the overall design for the success of the business. As an example, President Kennedy once visited the plant of the company producing rockets for the space program. He encountered a man sweeping the floor, and President Kennedy asked what the man was doing. His answer was, "Mr. President, I am helping to put a man on the moon!"

The initial draft should include

- The title of the SOP (what task does this SOP cover?);
- The reason for the SOP (why are we doing it, and why does it play a part in the overall success of the business?);

- The specific steps required to complete the task (describing the task in such a way that a person who has never done the task can complete the task without asking a single question—if that is not the result, then the SOP is not a success and needs to be revised).

As we go through the process, it's possible that additional items will be added. But for the draft, the above three items must be covered for the process to be a success.

To draft the document, it is a simple process. Think about having a conversation with the person, and you want to tell them how to do the task. This is exactly what you are doing. You are having a written conversation and covering every step of the process from inception to completion. Many find it helpful to insert photos into the document, the illustration of the task that photos may provide could be crucial to the person's ability to comprehend it over the written word. Adding some videos of the process can also be helpful showing a multi-step process. The goal is to illustrate the task completely, again eliminating the potential for questions to be raised as to the how or the why.

Keep in mind that someone reading the SOP may have never done the task before. The SOP should be written in a way so that someone completely unfamiliar with the task and resources should be able to complete it with no additional help.

CHAPTER 6
Management Review of the SOP

Once the draft of the SOP is complete, the manager must review it to make sure it thoroughly represents exactly how management wants the task done. The manager must be prepared to modify or delete information if required to make this a working document that can stand the test of time. The SOP must meet your approval. You are the manager, and you naturally have the final call.

An added benefit to writing and reviewing SOPs is taking a new look at your company. You might find out that employees have been doing tasks incorrectly for years. You might find out that they've discovered newer and more efficient ways of doing things. You might find areas of your business need more attention than you originally thought or areas where waste is rampant. This is such a great time to refamiliarize yourself with the strengths and weaknesses of your organization.

Often when this process is underway the manager sees that the present system has deviated over time and no longer performs as it was originally intended. The SOP writing process often reveals problems the manager may not even be aware of in the operating system of the company. The assembly of the library of SOPs provides an opportunity to review the entire operation in a way that has never been reviewed prior.

Do not shirk this part of the task; this is of utmost importance in the process of SOP preparation. Again, this is the responsibility of management, and the time invested now will pay huge dividends in the elimination of substandard processes that may exist in the business operation now.

CHAPTER 7

Submit the Document for Editing

After the document has been approved by management, it should be reviewed for correct language, proper presentation, and understandability. Have we given the SOP a proper title? Have we accurately identified the whys? Have we clearly stated the hows? At this point, the document should also be reviewed for proper wording and to make sure it is easy to understand. A goal is a procedure that can be easily comprehended by anyone requested to perform the task. Upon reading it, employees should now be able to complete the task without asking any questions.

It is critical that the language used is simple, clear, nontechnical, and easy for anyone to grasp. The task should be detailed in such a way that a new hire from another industry and another region can read it and complete the task.

As previously discussed, photographs are great additions to an SOP and can even further simplify the interpretation. Since learning styles of individuals vary, without the help of photos, many times SOPs miss the mark. Additionally, a great editor is important. During the editing process, you can easily determine if photos or even a video would enhance understanding for the end user. So, be prepared to add these if it is determined that it will enhance the SOP library to the level that is most effective.

Once this process is completed, the document should go back to the manager for review and confirm that it meets his or her needs and that the editing process has not removed any important steps.

As the manager, your role is key in much of this process. It's important not to let this pile up. Don't become the roadblock to the progress of the program. If you fail in your commitment to this, your team will become discouraged, and the project could get permanently sidetracked. If you exhibit it as not important to you by not moving promptly, then your team will pick up on the example you are setting for them and this will begin the defeat of the process. In other words, you are building the foundation for the success of the program, so dedicate whatever time it requires. Don't allow yourself to be the failure that will filter through your team. That's a poor example of leadership!

Remember, in the final analysis, you are going to save money, time, and resources once the program is fully implemented. It may just be the tool that affords you that time off, those vacations, and that quality time you dream of for other pursuits. After all, didn't you start the business to deliver the dreams you have in life? This may just be the vehicle that drives you to there!

CHAPTER 8
TEST THE SOP

How do you test an SOP? I suggest handing the SOP to a person who has never done the task to see if he or she can properly complete it as detailed without asking any questions. This could be assigned to a member of the company who does not presently do the task the SOP addresses. As an example, a sales clerk who is asked to do the shipping and receiving or a technician who could step in and do the payroll.

Testing tells you how the SOP will perform when put into practice. It's intended to be a document that stands the test of time, which means it will always work. However, future modifications might be necessary if changes happen within the business that requires a different approach. But, as the author of the SOP, you should endeavor to complete this document in the most usable, enduring, and practical form possible before it goes into use.

For the SOP to pass the test, the person must be able to:

- Start the task.
- Understand where to obtain the materials for the task.
- Know where and where the task is to be done.
- Complete the task in an orderly and effective manner.

CHAPTER 9

SUBMIT THE SOP TO YOUR TEAM MEMBERS

If you are working with a team, hand the SOP to your team members for review. If you don't have a team, you'll likely need someone else whose judgment you value to review the SOP for you. Explain to whoever reviews it that you want him or her to check for any issues with it that would make it unclear or incorrect.

You may ask, "If I don't have a team, why do I even need SOPs?" There are several reasons. One would be that you have plans to grow your business. In the future, you will likely have other people working for you who are assigned the task and will require direction. Another reason would be that you might want to sell the business someday and having clear operational guidelines would make that process much easier. Also, many individuals cannot properly proceed with tasks unless it is an orderly process. So, even as a one-man company, processes and systems will still be essential to creating more profits, less waste, and more sales.

As humans, we have processes that we adhere to daily; like it or not, most of us follow a daily regimen of operation. Likely every morning you follow a similar path: you get up at the same time, you do the same things, and you engage in the habits you have set for yourself. The purpose of the SOP is recording the proper and good daily habits so that the entire team can follow them. These are what we call habits, and maybe that is a term for the SOPs, it is an outline of the proper habits of the successful team and company.

This review process will also accomplish the goal of team buy-in since you have now likely involved them in the crucial steps of the process. This buy-in you've created will be essential as you implement these SOPs in your business model. Many times, the SOP will spell out a change in the way your team currently accomplishes a task. In this instance, the additional purpose is to break unproductive habits—ones counterproductive to the success of the business operation.

Here is the process for team review of the SOPs. First, distribute the SOP. Never distribute a large quantity of them at one time; I suggest a maximum of three if they are short, and if they are lengthy, you may want to distribute only one at a time. You do not want to overload your team with these. However, you do need to move on this promptly; you cannot wait for an indefinite time for their responses. You need to place a deadline on their replies. Give them 48 to 72 hours to submit to you in writing any suggested changes, questions, or modifications to the SOP.

However, I would also stress that if they do not reply in the time frame requested, you should presume the SOP is approved. But do remember that if you have team members who are not participating in the process, it may reveal a leadership or culture issue with your team. You need to find out why they are not participating. To create a truly useful SOP; it is important that the whole team provide input. If someone is not responding, it could indicate that the person is not a strong team member and may need more inspiration along these lines—or may need to be replaced.

Therefore, an additional part of the SOP process will involve gauging the present buy-in level of your team. As you go through the process, you will most likely discover who is onboard with you as a member of the team, and you may even uncover a rock star on your team. But you will also discover those who don't get it, making the process an eye-opening analysis of your team.

So, as you see, you have an additional benefit in this process, and that is a method by which you can measure the culture of the individuals on your team. This may just focus your attention on team members who do not possess the right individual culture to operate within your company culture. This is an additional benefit of a system of processes and procedures as it does alert you as to how the individual fits within the team framework.

CHAPTER 10

IMPLEMENTATION OF THE SOP

Once your team members have made their review of the SOP and you have modified, changed, or amended it as you see fit, it is time to start the process of implementation. Before implementation, I suggest that you add the following to the SOP:

- The date of implementation of the SOP
- Use of a numbering system for your SOP library (you should devise a filing system that will allow you to manage, modify, and amend the documents as you implement the processes into daily use)
- A line for individual team members to sign off on the SOP, indicating they've read it, understand it and approve it (this is for both existing team members and any new hires or others who may be assigned this task).
- Wording at the top of the sign-off sheet that says the following: "I have read this SOP and understand

[Margin note: Seek input from Ale manager]

that the company requires me to follow the SOP. In the event this SOP is not followed, I am fully aware that disciplinary action may be required. I agree to comply with any disciplinary action." (*I feel this kind of language is one way to signal to the team members the importance that you are placing on this process. You don't want to leave the impression that the use of this new procedure is optional*).

When an SOP is distributed, it is suggested that each one of signed by the team member who received it and that this signed document be entered into the employee's file that will confirm that each employee and has read the SOP and that they have agreed to comply. This will be an asset when disciplinary action is required.

This will provide you the data needed to keep track of which of your team members have received and signed off on each SOP. It will also be a basis for disciplinary action if that need should ever arise in the future. The systems you are building are the foundational blocks upon which you are structuring your business—in effect, a new company that will move you to the next level.

CHAPTER 11

DISTRIBUTION OF THE SOP

The SOP should be distributed to team members in a form they can access daily. This could be in a digital form, or in a notebook with printed sheets. Many companies will utilize both a printed and a digital format for employee guidance as required. It is key that the SOP is available to your team members for easy reference when needed. Furthermore, the SOP documents given to each employee should be audited on a regular basis to ensure they are cared for, are kept in the proper place, and are being followed.

Never distribute a library at one time, when the SOPs are distributed they should only be served in a method where they can be digested and understood by each of your team members. I suggest a short meeting with the following process:

- Call the team together.
- Explain the purpose of the short meeting.
- Distribute the documents you are implementing.

- Give a brief explanation of each.
- Ask if anyone has questions. If so, address these in a professional manner now.
- Request that if they discover an area or issue where the SOPs can be modified or otherwise amended to make them a better document then request they share this with you.
- Give the adoption date of the new policy.
- Ask your team for their help in making the program one of excellence.

CHAPTER 12

INSPECT FOR WHAT YOU EXPECT

A very important part of management is to inspect for what you expect. This inspection can be accomplished by you personally or by a person to whom you delegate this responsibility. This inspection happens without something going wrong (like a customer complaint). It is, in fact, what you do to prevent problems before they occur. Your job as the manager is to manage. That means more than simply resolving the issue when there is a complaint. It means anticipating issues and planning to head them off.

Even if you've delegated a task, it's your responsibility to follow up with that person to ensure it's being done properly. This is the leadership responsibility of inspection for what the leader expects, failure to do this will result in failed leadership. This is not micro-management, this is leadership. The failure of a person you have delegated something to should always be viewed as a failure of the leader in the delegation process. Leaders work with, inspire, encourage, and train others to follow processes. Failure to do this kind of follow-up, or failure to comply with your guidelines, invites chaos into your business, and chaos is a costly result to live with.

Inspection of the task completion, to our expectations, is often one of the leading failures for so many managers. They only look for expectation failure when something has gone awry. As the manager, it is a duty to do this periodic inspection, commit to doing this and you will find this will produce miraculous results with your team.

CHAPTER 13

WHAT DO I DO WHEN A MISTAKE HAPPENS?

Once a company has a library of SOPs, there will be three responses for any mistake. This is where the great manager sees a need for change and makes adaptations and modifications as the business matures and grows. The three answers to every mistake are the following:

There Is No SOP: This will be common, and unless the manager wants a career full of chaos, he or she will now start the SOP writing process to eradicate the chance that this will ever occur again in the future.

Someone Did Not Follow the SOP: The manager must now drill down on the reasoning and the solution. The first step is to look at the SOP. What is understandable, were our expectations realistic, and did we provide the tools and training to do the task? Whatever answers we find, what is our direction as the manager? This is all part of the process of growing a team of rock stars. They must be completely willing and able to do the task both mentally and physically. If they are not, then as leaders, we must take the required action.

The SOP is wrong: Often when a mistake happens as one researches the cause of the mistake, the answer could reveal that the SOP is flawed and does not properly present the process in a way it can be followed to reach the desired result(s). When the SOP is to blame, then the manager must step up with ownership of the mistake and the task guidelines reviewed and modified to one of accurate guidelines and procedures.

Once you have determined which of the three above reasons was the cause for the mistake, it is time to proceed with the needed corrective steps. If there is no SOP, then this is a future one we add to our "TO DO" list. Once a company is dedicated to a system of processes and procedures, the management will find that it will be a requirement for additional ones to be authored and added to the library.

If the cause is due to someone failing to follow the SOP, and in this search, we should investigate if the SOP is worded in a way that invites mistakes. Or, perhaps it lies in our training program. Did we properly train the person and provide them the needed tools to do the job? It may also signal an issue in our hiring processes. Are we hiring people who do not meet our actual criteria, and from this do we change our interview process to close the loopholes? You see, this is another benefit of the SOP process; it alerts us to many of the business weaknesses.

If the SOP is wrong, then we must take the steps of researching why it is wrong. Modify the SOP to cover the need, and implement an updated and upgraded SOP to cover the discrepancies.

CHAPTER 14
How do I Apply Disciplinary Action Using the SOP?

When there is a failure to follow the SOP by a team member you may be faced with the task of how to effectively counsel the team member and coach them to perfect the task. My suggested process is as follows:

- Access the SOP in your digital files that were not followed. This is one of the reasons for having all SOPs in a digital document for later use in various ways
- Upload the SOP to your desktop.
- Highlight the sections of the SOP the team member is not doing or completing to the description as the SOP details it.
- Insert the wording to describe what was done wrong by the team member at the end of the document in a different type style to make it stand out.

- Sign the form with your signature as the manager.
- Create a line on the document for the employee that reads as follows: "I have read the areas of this SOP that describe where I did not complete the task properly. I understand how I made this mistake, and I am committed to not repeating this mistake in the future."
- Have the team member sign and date the document, and insert it into his or her personnel file. If you must take more action, this serves as your documentation of warning the team member of his or her mistake and of any action that you may have to take in the future.
- You may even consider having a blank area where the team member can fill in how they plan to resolve the mistake from further repetition.

This is where the SOPs now work as a method of disciplinary action; SOPs also work as the basis of communication between the manager and the team member of resolution of issues.

Does this involve time? Most certainly it does! But in the long run, this is how you are going to build the strength of your team to the level you have envisioned.

CHAPTER 15

Ongoing Review and Suggested Modifications by Your Team Members

The best SOPs are ones that your team takes ownership of. In other words, they should feel free at any time, even after the SOP is in place, to suggest improvements, changes, or modifications to the SOP that will ensure better results for your customers and a smoother, less chaotic business operation.

The businesses with the best SOPs always have a team of people committed to the success of the project. This will also be a team with the right culture led by a vibrant management team. This is the making of a great company culture, driven by people with that as their personal culture.

To accomplish this, you will have to work with your team on the initial buy-in process. The formation of this was established at the beginning of the process. The team should realize, this is their document, this is their bible, this is their standard operating guidelines, and they have equal ownership in this. Making this a team ownership project, and not an ownership by management is going to drive the team spirit higher and higher and what you will find is that a team will be built that will self-police itself.

Once you have accomplished this, your job as a manager will change from working in the business to working on the business, and your time as a manager will be spent on building the successful strategies that take the business to a new level.

CHAPTER 16

Annual Management Review

As the manager, it is your responsibility to review the SOPs and the entire company on an annual basis. The following are questions the manager should ask in that annual review process:

- Is this SOP accurate and still doing the job?
- Have we changed a process that requires a modification or change to the SOP?
- Does some lack of customer satisfaction require that we change our system to better meet the needs of the customer?

You should have also had input from your team on an ongoing basis and if your meeting schedule is properly adhered to with the meeting process of tracking and measurement of the daily process, profit, mistakes, and fumbles, this makes the process a much easier process for you as the manager.

One of the business processes I promote in my coaching practice is the need for meetings. These meetings follow a schedule. Meetings properly planned and executed with a purpose, can go a long way in pinpointing the needs throughout the year, thereby making your annual SOP review much easier.

CHAPTER 17

Summaries of the SOPs

As you develop your SOPs, you will find that some will be very short and brief. These are simple to understand, comprehend and follow. But you will likely also compose some that may be large and bulky and hard to follow for that reason. Quite simply there will be a lot of details. When that situation arises, it is advised that you consider a summary of each large SOP.

The summary would be a much shorter condensed version of the SOP that is less than one page. It will include the key processes of the task; it will be helpful to add this step as it is a way to ensure easier comprehension of the task SOP.

CHAPTER 18

SECURITY OF THE SOP

Through this process, you have built a library of tremendous strength and value. You now need to take steps to ensure that each member of your team is aware that the SOPs are proprietary information and are not open to sharing with anyone else. This is a very important step. You have done piles of work; don't let someone take your hard work and simply use it to his or her advantage. In other words, take steps to protect your proprietary information.

SUMMARY AND CONCLUSIONS

SOPs and SOGs are tools for success, and business managers should invest the resources to create them. If they don't, they are at risk of continuing to operate in chaotic and unpredictable ways. Furthermore, without a properly defined and articulated system that assures consistency and clarity, waste will be a significant and regular outcome. Waste is what destroys your bottom line.

I encourage you to engage in the process described in this book, even though the journey may seem arduous. Let me assure you that if you are dedicated to the goal, you will find that once you get into the swing of the process, it gets much easier. I can also assure you that the return you will gain will be something that will lower your stress and give you back your life outside the world of business.

I want to thank you for taking the time to read this book. Let me know if I can help you in the process.

ABOUT THE AUTHOR

Jerry Isenhour is a business coach based in Charlotte NC who specializes in blue-collar home service contracting businesses. In his coaching and consulting practice he works in all areas of the country. His résumé also includes experience as the CEO of companies in service, retail, and manufacturing. Also, he has served as the president of national trade groups and education foundations, and on industry certification governing boards.

Jerry is a certified member of the John Maxwell Team as a leadership coach, teacher, and speaker. He is also a certified sales adviser with certification by Jeffrey Gitomer. He presently serves as the CEO and lead coach at CVC Coaching, a full-service coaching and consulting organization providing expertise to clients across the United States.

Jerry developed his thirst for the processes of SOPs and SOGs in his own service business after reading books and studies on how the military and successful business managers ran their businesses according to a strict system that controlled all operations. A part of this was his review of *The E Myth* by Michael Gerber and hearing the author speak. The value of the SOP process was quickly seen, and he began building SOPs/SOGs for his businesses, which included a chimney service company, a retail venture that sold specialty products for the outdoor living and fireplace industry, and a manufacturing company producing a product for the outdoor living industry.

During his time as the owner of various business endeavors, he also was highly involved in trade and educational groups on the state, regional, and national levels and has presented educational offerings to the industries he serves since 1984. Having trained thousands of business owners and technicians, he has become known as an expert in his fields.

In 2010, he became a coach and consultant to the industries in which he carried expertise, and today he works across the United States in his capacity as a teacher, coach, consultant, and educator. Even though he works with a wide variety of subject matters from both the technical and the operational side of the business, his true expertise as a systems expert has been one of his success foundations.

The first book authored by Jerry was titled *Chaos To Reinvention* and is the story of how the chaos disrupted his life and inspired him to become a coach for blue collar business owners and managers. Her is also a co-author of the books *The Daily Difference Life Lessons* & *Laying The Foundation For Your Dream Business*, both available on Amazon and other book sellers.

Strategies for Standard Operating Procedures was written when, after working as a coach and a consultant, it became increasingly clear that most managers, while wanting to implement a system of SOPs and SOGs, simply could not put together the process to make this happen. This book was authored to assist others in their pursuit of creating the perfect standard operating procedures and standard operating guidelines for their business models. But as the book details, it is not only important to know the method for writing these in a successful manner but also important to understand the process for communicating them so that your team buys in. The result is a company that is more committed to a culture of excellence, less waste, higher profits, and a great moral.

Jerry has also authored numerous items that have included journals, articles and is considered as a source of expertise on the subject matters he writes about and his coaching practice covers. He also prepares seminars, keynotes and talks on these subjects, and his audience is spread across the USA. His words, advice, counsel, and perspective are considered invaluable assets by many business owners.

To find out more about Jerry, visit his websites:

www.cvccoaching.com
www.jerryisenhour.com

Facebook: CVC Coaching
YouTube: CVCCoaching
Twitter: JerryCVC
Instagram: CVCJerry
Linkedin: Jerry Isenhour

Also tune into his podcast *The Blue Collar Success Network* on Soundcloud, Stitcher, and iTunes

If the process of writing your own SOPs is one that you want to do, but simply cannot get it done, then let's talk. One of the members of our team may be the person you need to help you get this task underway and to the process of implementation. We also have expertise on our team that can work on a consulting basis with you to make your SOP program a reality.

Feel free to contact Jerry. You can contact him through e-mail at jerry@cvccoaching.com. He will be glad to schedule a call with you to help you in your pursuit of the production of a library of SOPs and SOGs for your business.

Made in the USA
San Bernardino, CA
15 January 2020